7th Grade Middle School C

7th Grade
Middle School Chronicles

"Oh Essynce, if only you could see the future...."

Written by

Essynce E. Moore

write to:
Essynce Couture Publishing
P.O. BOX 5082
Hillside, NJ 07205

Printed in the United States of America
Published by Essynce Couture Publishing
Hillside, NJ 07205
Editor: Essynce Couture Publishing
Cover Photo: Essynce Moore
Cover Design: Jamar Hargrove – Owner of NeedGFX.com
Essynce E. Moore
Entrepreneur, Motivational Speaker, Actress, Author, Fashion Designer & Stylist, Founder and CEO of Essynce Couture, LLC, Essynce Couture University, and Essynce Couture Spa and Boutique

www.essyncecouture.com

ISBN-13: 978-0692651537
Printed in USA by Essynce Couture Publishing

Essynce E. Moore

Dedicated to that kid at the skating rink who loved my first book and told me I needed to write a book for every year I'm in school for the rest of my life. You inspired me kid.

Table of Contents:

Introduction

Introduction:

You can only expect so much from the world, your friends, and yourself. Eventually, you will grow into the habit of expecting things a certain way, shape, or form. I always knew to expect the unexpected simply because of all the surprises the world had shocked me with.

Like when I developed a crush during my 7th grade year on a guy I had nearly nothing in common with or when I became an entrepreneur when I was only 10 years old. My whole life so far had been filled with a series of unexpected events. Therefore, I had chosen to accept the fact that you can only expect so much from the world, your friends, and middle school.

Read on as I go through my 7th grade year, walking blindly towards the frycken future. Oh and one more thing my famous word "fryck" is back!

Essynce E. Moore

Chapter 1:
"Re-united!"

Chapter 1
"Re-united!"

My first day of 7th grade was...average. I wore a skirt, school shirt, high knee socks, and 1 inch wedges (that was literally the only time I wore the actual school uniform during the school year).

I guess you can say my friends and I "re-united" but the reunion wasn't much of a big deal because during the summer time, in August, for my birthday I invited most of my friends to go celebrate my b-day with me at Splash Zone, a really cool water park in New York. Anyway, for most of the day I simply hugged some friends I hadn't seen in a while and I managed to get to all of my classes without getting lost. Now for that I deserve a pat on the back because if you read my first book then you'd know that last year I got so lost on my first day to the point where I almost cried...I know, embarrassing right. Looking past that and re-zooming to this year I also met my new teachers who were pretty cool I guess...I mean how cool can a teacher really get?

Speaking of teachers I greeted some of my old ones from last year. It seemed kind of strange though, seeing them was kind of like a flashback to a "simpler" time. Also known as 6th grade.

After a couple of months, since the first day everyone and everything seemed to be going pretty smoothly, being me I hoped things would stay that way...little did I know there would soon be a day when a boy would call me bae...

Notes:

_____

_____

_____

_____

_____

_____

_____

_____

_____

_____

_____

_____

Chapter 2:

"Man-Thongs for Essynce Couture."

Chapter 2:
"Man-Thongs for Essynce Couture."

- Science Class

- First Period

- He Called Me Bae

Unfortunately, I can't remember how he put it in a sentence or how it sounded when it left his lips, because at the time I thought nothing of it. After all, this was the kid who spoke to me for the first time last year, suggesting that I make and sale man-thongs for Essynce Couture. Yes, you read correctly. Man. Thongs. Back then I considered him my mortal enemy because he'd hit me all the time for no reason but even I'm forced to admit the kid was funny... I mean come on "man-thongs," who says that?! When he first brought it up I laughed and kindly rejected his suggestion and he actually seemed pretty bummed about it.

From this point on I will refer to "the kid" as "The Flame" because flames can do one of two things, either make you warm or make you burn and "the kid" I mentioned earlier did both...however we don't find out why and how till later on, but believe me what's to come is worth the wait and the read.

Weeks had gone by and he still called me bae, however I just looked at him as a friend...not even as a friend...as a kid who flirted with me and I tolerated him.

I remember, on a Friday, my friend Mia had gotten permission from her mom to spend the night at my house, so after school we walked to my house which was only about 15 minutes away from the school. Once we got there we changed out of our uniform and put on a casual outfit. Mia wore an off the shoulder shirt with jeans and sneakers, while I wore an oversized pink hoodie with leopard print leggings and pink sneakers. My hair was pulled back and I had my Essynce Couture pink lipstick on that I wore to school earlier.

About a half-an-hour after we were dressed Mia and I had decided to go to the PAL, in other words, the Community Center. It's literally 5-10 minutes away from my house depending on how fast you walk and usually a lot of people from my school and other schools go...especially on Fridays. When we were half way there Mia brought up this guy she liked.

She told me that he was cute, an 8th grader, and that she thought he liked her back because he always flirted with

7

her. A couple minutes passed and I could see the PAL in a distance. I felt a slight push on my shoulder and looked to the one who had pushed me, Mia. She gestured to the boy a few feet away and quietly whispered "that's him."

I looked to where her finger pointed and eyed the guy up and down. I had seen him in school before and we had only spoken once when he asked me about my business (Essynce Couture), he thought it was pretty cool.

Anyway his name's Sean and even though he wasn't my type, he seemed to definitely be Mia's. He went inside the PAL after saying hey to Mia and I. However we went to the playground area and met up with a couple of our friends who were on the swings. One of my friends, Angel, who I had known for years but we never really talked because we were in different "groups", complimented my outfit and I said thanks. We all talked for a while till we finally decided to go to the play structure.

We talked there for a bit about random topics that we would probably forget after a day or two, and about 10 minutes later "he" walked in...The Flame walked in.

Notes:

_____

_____

_____

_____

_____

_____

_____

_____

_____

_____

_____

Essynce E. Moore

Chapter 3:
"This is my bae."

Chapter 3:
"This is my bae."

As soon as "he" saw me a smirk formed on his face and him and a couple of his friends started to make their way toward us. I recognized the two guys that were with him but at this point I honestly don't even remember what they looked like...I just remember "him." The Flame sat by me, on one of the steps that lead to the slide, and we all talked for a while about more random stuff and soon enough a girl who looked to be in high school came in. She seemed to know The Flame and before she began speaking to him she said hi to all of us. She looked between him and I, probably noticing how close we were sitting and she smirked before The Flame could say anything.

"This is my bae." He said smiling, looking at the girl, then at me. At some point when I was still processing the words that he had just used to introduce me, he had managed to throw his arm over my shoulder.

"So she's your girlfriend?" The girl asked, seeming slightly amused by my speechless state that I seemed to be vacationing in.

Finally, when I had come back to humanity I responded before The Flame could.

"No, but he's cute so I let him get away with calling me that." I shrugged, scooting slightly away from him.

She chuckled and nodded in understanding, however in that moment I realized something. I realized how comfortable I really was with his arm around me...I realized that I had begun to fall for The Flame. Not my absolute best move...

Now this may sound like your typical, everyday crush, but I wasn't and still am not your typical, everyday person. I didn't like having crushes, till this day I still don't, I mean they're called a "crush" for a reason right? I also didn't like the idea of someone having the ability to make me do things that I wouldn't normally do. For example, making me blush. It's so cliché and cheesy. I found it cute when other people did it but not when my crush made me do it. Then again, I thought, could having a crush really be that bad? Oh, Essynce, if only you could see the future.

Notes:

_____

_____

_____

_____

_____

_____

_____

_____

_____

_____

_____

Chapter 4:

"...go chop your hair off."

Chapter 4:
"...go chop your hair off."

I've always known that I was different then everyone else. I knew that my interests were different. I knew that my "risks" were different.

One of my unique risks involved my hair. I had wanted to get the side of it shaved for two years but my dad always said no. Finally, when I was 11 he told me to ask him when I turned 12 and I did. After having a debate with him about all the pros and cons with getting my hair shaved I had gotten him to say yes...well not exactly. His exact words were along the lines of "Fine, go chop your hair off" and honestly that was all I needed to hear.

It was the perfect timing too because my cousin had gotten permission from her mom to get the side of her hair shaved as well. So on October 31, 2014, while children were trick-or- treating their hearts out, my aunt was shaving the side of my head.

That Friday was literally one of the most exciting and scariest Fridays I've ever experienced. I couldn't even wait till Monday to show off my new hairstyle. Sure I had brought up the idea of getting the side of my hair shaved to my friends before but I don't think any of them actually thought I'd do it. Even I didn't think I'd do it.

That Monday I actually looked forward to going to school...for once. Everyone had different opinions about my hair. Some people liked it, some were confused by it, and then there were those few who had no words. I, however, was amused by everyone's responses and curious expressions. I was curious myself as to why everyone paid so much attention to something that had no effect on their lives. Why make such a big deal about something that had nothing to do with them? I shaved my hair for me. Yeah, there were some people who didn't like my hair. But guess what: My hair didn't like them either.

Notes:

_____

_____

_____

_____

_____

_____

_____

_____

_____

_____

_____

Chapter 5: "The truth is..."

Chapter 5:
"The truth is..."

Now-a-days the internet is everything and knows everyone...including The Flame, who happened to comment on one of my Instagram pictures, telling me to hit him up. Being the innocent victim of a crush that I was, I couldn't even deny the retarded butterflies that I felt in my stomach when he commented. From that point on every time I'd text him and my phone would buzz, I'd feel those same butterflies...I liked him that much.

By the time these events were taking place I had told most of my friends that I liked him, some of the mutual friends I had with him, and I even told my mom. Part of me told them hoping that they'd tell him and I could stop beating around the bush, however the other part of me was hoping that they wouldn't bring it up to him at all.

Anyway you're probably wondering why I told so many people that I like him, even if they were my friends and the truth is growing up I've realized that a lot of people, including myself, always keep their crushes a secret. I on the other hand hated doing that, I did it, but I didn't like doing it. I mean we spend so much time wondering if they like us back that we end up losing ourselves trying to find an answer that doesn't take much to get.

They say curiosity killed the cat, luckily for anyone who's capable of reading this you're not a cat, and I don't think your crush finding out you like them is gonna kill you...hopefully not. And come on, what are the odds, three things can happen.

A. Your crush likes you back, you get married, have ten kids and name them all Essynce...because come on, that's an awesome name

B. Your crush doesn't like you back but you whine up with your "true love" eventually and have kids all named Essynce (Because once again I say it, it's an awesome name)

C. You're like me and you write a book about how 7th grade basically put you on a roller coaster that made you wanna puke...like a lot... (By the way, Essynce is still an awesome name)

Anyway, my point is if you like someone I think you should just go for it and tell them, and if you're too embarrassed or scared to tell them in person be old school and write them a note. I, myself think that's a cute gesture. Then again I like anything that expresses the way people feel through writing.

In late January, I invited some friends of mine to go ice-skating with me, to celebrate the launching of my first book 6th Grade Middle School Chronicles. The friends being CeCe, Alex, Jacky, Zach, Jack, and The Flame. Now that I think about it, I think it's kind of funny because at the time everyone but The Flame knew I liked him. My friends would purposely push me closer to him or when we were skating we all held hands and decided to skate together, of course they tried to make The Flame and I hold hands. But that didn't really work out so we all just skated off in our own directions. Till this day The Flame still teases me about how he was able to ice skate faster than I, being that I have more experience ice skating. I just laugh and argue with him about how he's faster because he has more experience regularly skating, which isn't that different from ice skating.

When we left the skating rink my mom took us back to my house and we all watched movies on the couch, with a large blanket, and two pillows that we consistently fought over. Of course my friends practically forced me to sit next to The Flame but I didn't mind.

Before the movie started, Jack took my phone and then he took The Flame's. What he did next was childish and kind of amusing. He took our phones and made it look like we were texting each other. He took my phone and texted The Flame's phone asking "Do you wanna go out?" Then he used The Flame's phone to text back "Sure." When we got our phones back we looked to see what Jack had done. After reading the messages The Flame smirked and – having only a small percentage of "dating" experience that I have – I was speechless and confused. The thoughts that ran through my head made me seem like an immature five-year-old who had just shared a cookie with her crush.

Did this mean that we were dating? Did that smirk mean that he likes me ba...? "Don't worry Essynce I was just kidding," Jack said, bringing me out of my thoughts. "Oh," was my only response.

If you haven't noticed a lot of times I tend to overthink things. Even little things. It's a habit of mine that I've been trying to get rid of.

Anyway, eventually when we moved past that slightly awkward moment, we had a good time and writing about that moment right now, I feel like I get to relive it all over again. I remember during the movie I would play with The Flame's hair, while CeCe sprung her legs across my lap, and would purposely put her feet in The Flame's face...which made us all laugh.

That Sunday night when my mom dropped all of my friends off to their homes I texted The Flame and he asked me a question. He told me that Jack, who was good friends with him, told him that I liked him and he asked me was that true. At the time my heart was beating ridiculously fast, my palms were sweaty, and the only thought that was registering in my mind was "tell him" and I did.

I asked him who he liked and he asked me, "Who do you think?"

My response was, "I won't know for sure till you tell me." That's when he said he liked me...The Flame liked me back!

That was one of the many nights I couldn't sleep because he was on my mind.

Notes:

_____

_____

_____

_____

_____

_____

_____

_____

_____

_____

_____

Essynce E. Moore

Chapter 6:

"Going out with one of your friends..."

Chapter 6:
"Going out with one of your friends..."

It had been about two weeks since The Flame and I admitted to liking each other. By now it was the beginning of February and it was also the beginning of new relationships. Now that I think about it I wonder if Valentine's Day had anything to do with it....maybe all the heart decorations and chocolates were getting into some people's heads.

Anyway, since ice-skating not much had changed. The Flame and I still acted the same around each other and I had begun tutoring my best friend, Chris. Tutoring him was really fun actually. It was like hanging out with the older brother I never had, and I even got paid by his mom, who was like my aunt. It was a "win-win" for everyone in my perspective.

The only thing that bugged me was sometimes when I

tutored Chris he'd talk about his 6th grade girlfriend or ask me for advice, and at first I didn't mind. I mean that's what best friends are for right, giving each other advice, helping each other out? But after a while I guess you can say I got jealous. Then again I always do when my best friends get in relationships, Chris, Zach, and Amy. I can be pretty possessive sometimes and a lot of times I just like keeping my best friends to myself, and if they get hurt then I get hurt and I don't like when I get hurt...so the person who hurt my best friend and I better be ready for double the revenge.

It was either a Monday or a Wednesday when I found out that The Flame had just begun dating my friend, Alice. I remember because it was at the beginning of the week and it was Mondays and Wednesdays that I tutored Chris. It was after school and I was walking towards my mom's car, where Chris would meet me so we could go to my house to begin our tutoring session. That's when Jack had jumped in front of me, out of no-where and asked "would you be upset if you found out The Flame was dating one of your friends?"

I was completely caught off guard by the question and I continued walking towards my mother's car, with Jack trailing behind me. The question came so far out of no-where that I ended up shouting 3 random answers over the loud group of my peers that happened to pass us.

"Yes! No! I don't know!"

Jack looked confused by my sudden outburst and he also looked as if he knew something I didn't.

"Why do you ask anyway?" I asked. I wasn't completely oblivious to why he might've asked, obviously The Flame might have just gotten himself a girlfriend but at the end of the day I still didn't know for sure.

"The Flame is going out with one of your friends," and as if what he said hadn't just stopped my heart and my entire figure for a moment he asked "Can I go over your house today?"

"Sure" was my only response and we both had finally gotten into my mom's car, where Chris awaited us already in the back seat.

When we got to my house my mother went to her room and the rest of us settled down in the living room, watching the cartoons that I had put on the TV. (If you know me then you know I have a huge obsession with watching cartoons)

Chris and I decided that I'd begin tutoring him in about an hour, so we both had some time to relax first and not to long afterwards my mom had told me to do the dishes. I was too lost in my own thoughts to even put up an argument. Chris and Jack were too lazy to help me with the dishes so while I scrubbed only god knows what off of a plate they got to watch "Fairly Odd Parents"...lucky frycks.

As I played cheesy, old school music off of my phone and began scrubbing the forks and knifes I thought about what Jack had previously said over and over again.

"The Flame is going out with one of your friends."

So many thoughts were rushing through my head at once and the angelic voice of John Stamos, coming from my phone, began to drown out.

I guess he didn't like me that much after all.

Stop being so negative, you're better than that...

But-

Stop!

It was like I was having an internal battle with myself, like how in school we'd try to figure out how in a story if the conflict was man vs universe, man vs man, or, in my case, girl vs self.

That was when suddenly a new thought came to mind...

Who was the "friend" that The Flame was going out with?

I was finishing up on the last few dishes I had when I decided I'd ask Jack who the "lucky girl" was, and just like that, Jack happened to come in the kitchen, not to help me with the dishes, but instead to criticize my music.

"Essynce,...what are you listening to?" he chuckled and I could tell that he was trying to hold in an outburst of laughter.

By now I had come back to reality and that's when my favorite old school song of all time registered in my ears.

31

"Stand By Me by Ben E. King." Was my response, and for that brief second The Flame seemed to slip my mind and was replaced by the sweet lyrics of Stand By Me.

"If the sky that we look upon should tumble and fall...
Or the mountains should crumble to the sea...
I won't cry, I won't cry
No I won't shed a tear...
Just as long as you stand, stand by me"

That's when Jack had taken my phone and changed the song to something more "this generation." Nicki Minaj echoed from my phone and I looked at Jack and frowned. Not that I had anything against Nicki, I just wasn't in the mood for her music.

After all, I had just found out that my crush was dating one of my friends and then suddenly the memory was back and I asked Jack the obvious question.

"Who is The Flame dating?" He looked slightly shocked at first by the coming of no-where question, and then he became hesitant to tell me and that's when he said it, her name, one of the girls I'd least expect would have anything to do with it.

"Alice."

Notes:

_____

_____

_____

_____

_____

_____

_____

_____

_____

_____

_____

Essynce E. Moore

Chapter 7:
"...pants and shorts..."

Chapter 7:
"...pants and shorts..."

Alice. Of all people...Alice. This was the girl I hugged and greeted every day and I never suspected it to be her. Now don't get me wrong Alice is awesome and so gorgeous in her own unique way, I just didn't expect it to be her. Alice and The Flame were just so...different, and not the kind of "opposites attract" kind of different but more of the "pants and shorts" different.

It sounds confusing but think about it this way, the opposite of pants is a shirt but instead of The Flame and Alice being pants and shirts, they were pants and shorts...similar but very different. Leave it to me to make a fashion or clothing reference no matter what the circumstance is.

Anyway, I don't know maybe it's just the jealousy talking because even at this point I can still remember the envy and anger I felt in that moment and I'm almost embarrassed by it. Almost being the operative word because at the end of the day I know now that I'm not the only one in the world who sometimes feels that way.

Call me a creep but I even remember exactly how many days they dated...6, and I know because in the matter of those 6 days Alice's Instagram bio went from 'married' to 'divorced.'

Now that I think about it, it was never really the days that mattered, it was what happened in the gist of them. During those 6 days The Flame and I didn't speak to each other once. We acted as if we had never even made contact with one-another, it was complete and utter avoidance. There was no eye contact made, nothing at all...only the hurt I felt, that made direct contact with my heart every time I looked at him...because every time I looked at him I was reminded of Alice, his girlfriend.

I told my mom about what happened and I even told her a little bit about how I felt. However I didn't want to tell her too much because I knew she wouldn't think it was a big deal but at the time it was a big deal to me. My mom told me that 10 years from now none of it would even be or seem important...it would be the last thing on my mind, but the truth is, in that moment, I wasn't thinking about what life would be like 10 years from then. I was thinking about how I felt in that moment...in that single, individual moment, and I was hurt...and mad.

I wasn't necessarily mad at Alice, we didn't have any classes together so we never really got the chance to talk like we used to, plus I never even told her that I liked him. Also, I wasn't necessarily mad at The Flame either, I was mostly

37

mad at myself. Mad that I gave him the power to convince me the sky was green and he couldn't have cared less, mad that I let everyone convince me that "we were going to end up together" when really he had another girl on his mind all along, and you know what I was even mad at him because all along he had me thinking that he liked me when really he didn't...or so I thought.

Notes:

Essynce E. Moore

Chapter 8:

"The idea of him..."

Chapter 8:
"The idea of him..."

It had been two days since Alice and The Flame broke up and in the afternoon, at school that day, at lunch something that hadn't happened in a while happened...he talked to me. However I was mad at him and when he called my name from the lunch table he was sitting at, behind me, I pretended I didn't even hear him. I was giving him the silent treatment because at the end of the day I always thought that the most dangerous thing you could say was nothing...oh the irony.

Anyway when he realized that I was intentionally ignoring him he started yelling my name as if we were miles away from each other, when in reality we were only a small gap away from one-another. He even resolved to getting his friends and even Jacky, who happened to be MY friend to send messages telling me that he was sorry and "all that jazz." However his humorous side didn't leave him once because every time I'd turn around to look at him he'd pretend to cry and he'd beg for my forgiveness. His friends and Jacky would laugh and I would try not to and that basically went on for the rest of lunch.

That night I received a text from The Flame himself. He had texted me asking if I was still mad at him and I told him no, because I honestly wasn't. Sure I wasn't as fond of him as I used to be but I wasn't necessarily mad at him either. Till this day I still realize that it was in that moment that my feelings for him decreased...just a bit...because like I said before I don't like it when I get hurt, and when I get hurt I become very protective of myself and I end up trying to prevent the cause of the hurt originally from hurting me again. I guess it was just my body's way of protecting myself both mentally and physically.

That same month I happened to get asked out 3 times, by 3 different guys and I felt kind of bad for rejecting each and every one of them because in some weird way I felt that I could relate to them. Out of the 3 guys there were two in my grade and 1 kid in 8th grade who I never really talked to except for one time on Instagram. His name was Jaden and till this day he still is pretty mean to me sometimes and I think it has something to do with the rejection, but truth be told I don't really care. The other guys and I decided to just be friends so that was something that not only worked out but I also cared about.

It was the month of March at this point and that happened to be the month that I began talking to this 8th grader in my school, Jace. He had given me a really sweet to be honest on Instagram and we wound up texting each other quite often. Now before you begin jumping to conclusions I didn't like him in that way, we were only friends, but as a week had gone by I developed a small crush on him and I told him. Don't get me wrong I was nervous but I told him anyway. At the time I did like The Flame more...and even though this does sound cheesy The Flame seemed to have topped everyone I've ever liked. (I can already see the cocky grin that's going to be on his face when he reads that...) Then again I hadn't liked someone before The Flame since I was like 8.

Anyway, after I told Jace I liked him we remained as friends and I guess it hurt a little at first but it wasn't him not liking me back that hurt. It was the idea of him not liking me back that stung a little, not to sound conceited or anything but I guess you could say I was just used to people liking me and it was a little out of the ordinary for me when they didn't. But in life not everyone is going to like you and now I know that. I got over Jace a couple weeks later but till this day I guess you can say I still have a small soft spot for him, I think it has something to do with his eyes, his beautiful hazel-green eyes,...I'll get over it though...hopefully.

Notes:

_____

_____

_____

_____

_____

_____

_____

_____

_____

_____

Essynce E. Moore

Chapter 9: "Spring Break!"

Chapter 9:
"Spring Break!"

Eventually, April came around and it was finally the 10 days of freedom everyone had been waiting for...spring break! During spring break my mom and I had decided to go to Georgia, for a couple reasons actually. One reason being I had an event down there, two my mom wanted to look at some of the houses they had there, and three for fun!

My mom said I could invite one friend, since she didn't want me to be the only kid, since her boyfriend, Michael was going. At first I thought of inviting my friend, Alex. I thought it would be easier since our moms already knew each other plus Alex was just really cool to hang out with, but she wasn't able to go due to her dad saying no. It was literally a few days before we'd be heading off to Georgia and I told my mom that since Alex couldn't go I'd be inviting Alice.

At the time my mom already knew Alice pretty well because she'd started coming over my house often, but she didn't know Alice's mom so she wasn't sure Alice would be able to get permission to go, so to be on the safe side my mom called CeCe's mom and invited CeCe to accompany us on our trip. By the time my mom told me that she invited CeCe Alice's mom spoke to my mother and had given permission for Alice to come. That's how Alice's mom and my mom began talking, and wound up becoming good friends.

We were all going to be spending a week together in Georgia and at the end of the day I think we all had a little fun. We went shopping, swimming, and we even built a fort made out of blankets and pillows, in the room at my mom's friend's house that we were staying in. I recorded and made videos of everything we did for the entire week, while we were there.

Alice and I finally got to talk more like we used to and we even got to discussed matters concerning The Flame. She told me how she really didn't know that I liked him when they were dating and I told her I didn't blame her for anything. Since Alice was over him (unlike me she gets over people very quickly) she encouraged me to go out with him but I wasn't so sure about that.

It was that trip that CeCe and Alice became like sisters to me. Sure, we got on each other's nerves every once in a while, and CeCe might have had an incident involving a broken bed and an angry Michael but now I love those girls more than ever.

A couple of days after we first arrived in Georgia, The Flame and I started texting one- another. It was in that week apart that we started to get to know each other for real this time.

It'd be 3 in the morning when we'd be talking about all the things we never talked about before. I'd ask him random questions, like how many kids he wanted to have or who his celebrity crush was and he'd text me back faster than he used to, actually seeming eager to talk to me. Till this day I still remember what his answers to those questions were too...

And the later it'd get the more personal our conversations got. We'd begin talking about our feelings for one-another and all the other cheesy romance clichés. Looking back at that moment now...it's all just a memory, a memory I can't decide whether or not I should forget. In school everyone saw him as "the bad boy," the one who always got in trouble but to me he was so much more than that.

You see to me he was never a troubled kid or someone who couldn't walk away from a problem correctly...he was a perfect storm...with gallons of rain and sparks of lightning, and I wanted him to be my own perfect disaster. I was completely infatuated with him...and now that I think about it maybe that was the problem.

Eventually, I got tired of beating around the bush and I finally asked him why he hadn't asked me out yet and apparently he thought I wasn't ready. Now that I think about it I wasn't and even though I hate to admit it he was right...I was not ready. My mom was always on my mind, my career was always on my mind, but the one thing I don't think he ever understood was he was always on my mind too.

Notes:

_____

_____

_____

_____

_____

_____

_____

_____

_____

_____

_____

_____

Essynce E. Moore

Chapter 10: "Problems"

Chapter 10:
"Problems"

A couple weeks after we came back from spring break a few problems arose and they weren't all mine for once.

Apparently, one of the problems had to do with my best friend, Amy and her boyfriend. The rumor wheel was rolling around and a tale began to spread that Amy's boyfriend was cheating on her with one of the 6th graders. I had left school early that day due to a dentist appointment I had and I didn't find out what was going on till Amy's boyfriend texted me after school that day. He was whining about how Amy believed the rumor and how it wasn't true at all, and he didn't really have my attention until he said the one thing that made something in me put all my attention on him and that conversation.

"Amy was crying."

Now it may not sound like a big deal but if you know my best friend than one thing you know for sure is she does not cry. Amy is one of the strongest people I know, she doesn't get all "lovey-dovey heartbroken" easily. In fact in our 7 years of friendship I had only seen her cry once, in 3rd grade. So you could only imagine my moment of shock when my best friend's boyfriend told me that she was crying. Immediately, I felt guilty that I wasn't there when my best friend needed me most, and to make it even worse I had even gotten a text from other friends saying that Amy was looking for me in school.

So the next day at school I spoke to Amy about what happened and she almost cried again but I wouldn't let her, she's better than that. Eventually, her and her boyfriend, who I never quite understood why she liked him worked things out and continued their "happy couple" lifestyle.

That's when more problems seemed to arise concerning Alice, Mia, and my friend Taylor. It all started when Mia and Taylor liked each other and told me about their feelings for one-another. They both knew that the other liked them back and being me I decided to play one of my favorite games, Cupid! So I sharpened my arrows, aimed my bow, and shot them both in the butt! However, I must have shot an additional person by accident because a few days after they began going out someone else seemed to have their eyes on Taylor, and her name was Alice.

Apparently, Alice had been flirting with Taylor, who used to have a small crush on her. Alice and Mia were friends and I never did find out if Alice knew that Taylor was taken at the time but I guess it doesn't really matter now because after a couple weeks Mia and Taylor broke up...yeah not much of a happy ending, huh?

However these series of problems aren't ending just yet. That same week as I was walking to my last period class in the hallway, I saw Chris with multiple people crowded around him as he was about to cry. From what I heard them saying Chris's girlfriend had just broke up with him. Being the over protective best friend that I was and still am I pushed the crowd out of my way and knelt down, against one of the lockers, next to him. His hands were covering his face and when I tried to talk to him he didn't hear me due to all the yelling voices from the crowd either asking or teasing him about the break up. I knew there was no use of me staying there and being late to my class so I went upstairs, to my classroom, but when I got in there all I could do was think about Chris.

My best friend was upset and I left him. The thought ended up consuming me with so much regret and guilt that I spoke to my teacher, Mr. Jackson about going to talk to Chris, who he knew was my best friend. He had given me permission and went to Chris's class himself and spoke to Chris's teacher, convincing her to let me talk to him. Chris walked out of his classroom with his head down and Mr. Jackson had told me to take as long as I wanted to speak to Chris...I found a new respect for Mr. Jackson that day. Anyway, I spoke to Chris and he didn't hesitate when it came to opening up to me about what was really going on. Truth be told, I knew Chris well and I knew that even though he did over exaggerate sometimes he didn't just cry over anything.

He told me all the things that had got him down, things

about his parents, things about his brother, and things about what everyone seemed to already know...his girlfriend...well ex- girlfriend. I told Chris about some of my past and current problems as well, and we kind of just had a moment...a brother and sister moment, because he wasn't just my best friend he was my brother. When Chris started to feel better we went back to class, with literally about 20 minutes to spare till the school day was over.

Little did I know the problems in the school were faaarrr from over...

Apparently Jacky was having a few problems herself, problems involving a girl and a boy...big mistake. See what I've learned in my 12 years of existence is that when one boy is with two girls, even if they're all friends a problem is bound to happen at some point. The problem can have something to do with the girls intensively debating with the guy or the guy dating both the girls...or we could just have the whole Mia, Alice, and Taylor thing all over again... but in Jacky's case it was none of the above.

Jacky's problem consist of her "friend" going out with her crush,...I'm getting a sense of déjà vu here. However, the difference between my past situation and Jacky's is her "friend" knew that Jacky liked the guy, and boy did she like him a lot. Jacky told me about what happened and I asked her what I thought was a simple question, yet it was a question that seemed to catch her slightly off guard.

"So are you mad at this "friend" of yours?"

She hesitated at first but then responded by explaining to me that she wasn't in fact mad at the girl who had a part in the new relationship but instead she was mad at the guy, who knew that Jacky liked him. And if I'm correct I do believe he liked Jacky back...either that or all his text messages to her on KIK were just a big, fat lie. Then again, that's not even the point. The point is that to me it made no sense as to why Jacky could be so easily mad at the guy and so "easy going" with her "friend," the girl. I guess looking at things from my point of view I just saw it as kind of messed up that Jacky was going to be mad at the guy but not the girl because at the end of the day a relationship takes two people to follow through with and no one was threatening Jacky's little "friend" saying that she had to go out with the guy, it was her choice.

But you know what, it was and still isn't my business, its Jacky's. However she did sort of make it my business when that night I received a text from her asking if she got in a fight with the girl, who she thought was her friend, would I jump in...

Finally, towards the end of the cave of problems, when I saw the light at the end of the tunnel and thought I made it out alive, thought I was home free my problem came to be. I remember it being a Thursday when I was told by Jack that The Flame had gotten himself a girlfriend...again.

Notes:

_____

_____

_____

_____

_____

_____

_____

_____

_____

_____

_____

Essynce E. Moore

Chapter 11:
"Just take someone's phone and you guys are basically best friends"

Chapter 11:
"Just take someone's phone and you guys are basically best friends"

It was during lunch, when Jack had told me...

Why is it always Jack who's telling me?

Anyway, I was sitting next to The Flame, with Zach on the opposite side of me and that was when out of the blue Jack said it...

"Essynce, did you know that The Flame has a girlfriend in Union?" Everyone, who was sitting at that lunch table went silent and not just any silent, drop a feather and you could still hear it silent.

Jack said it so casually as if no one there knew that I liked The Flame, when in reality everyone there did...I think the entire 7th grade knew.

I'm not mad at Jack though, he meant no harm, what I am

mad about though was that when he said that the first thing I did was look to The Flame...pretty pathetic, don't you think? I guess there was a part of me that was hoping he'd tell Jack to "stop playing" or "that was your worst joke yet" but those words never came out of his mouth.

When I looked towards the boy I had fallen so hard for he didn't even look at me, his attention was on Jack and he glared at him as if he were mad at what Jack had just told me...I guess I wasn't supposed to know.

That day I didn't go home feeling pain or hurt, I felt only two emotions. I either felt numb or anger. I guess I just trusted The Flame to not hurt me again. That's something I've recently discovered about myself...I trust too easily. I used to assume that if I don't hurt people they won't hurt me but that's not true. People may try to hurt you countless of what you do or what you've done to, or for them, and even though that sucks it's the painful truth. A good friend once told me that the truth is very belligerent by nature. Man was he right...

The next day, I guess you can say I wanted to rip The Flame's head off, but unfortunately there were too many witnesses at school and I resolved to just ignoring him, while throwing in a few glares every so often. At lunch I didn't sit at the table with him and Zach like I usually did, but I did stop by there to make sure Zach ate something. For some reason I never understood, Zach would never eat very much at lunch, so I'd have to make sure he did. So while I was talking to Zach about eating something or offering to buy him something from the vending machine The Flame came with his food and sat by him. He tried speaking to me but I just gave him a look that could kill...literally. It was the look I give when I'm seriously mad and not a joking or playful kind of mad but straight face, I really want to hurt you kind of mad.

Zach looked slightly shocked, he wasn't used to me acting that way towards The Flame or anyone for that matter. I was usually that peppy person who would always smile or playfully stick her tongue out at someone. Anyway, The Flame was used to me talking to Zach about eating something and he knew that Zach was my best friend so like the caring person who I once thought he was he gave Zach half his sandwich, then looked at me. I looked at him for a brief second and then looked back at Zach. You see my natural instinct would have been to thank him for helping me out with Zach but...I wasn't exactly fond of him in that moment. Zach, who was kind of oblivious to what was really going on said, "See, now I have something to eat."

"Just let me know if you get hungry after you finish that," I said and then walked away.

I didn't know who to talk to about how I felt or what I should do, but then it hit me and I spoke to the only person who's managed to tolerate what I considered problems for 12 (soon to be 13) years. I told my mom and she didn't tell me that I was "only 12" or ask me if I really considered that to be a problem. Instead she gave me advice. My mom told me to do my own thing and don't focus on just him and she even suggested that I remain friends with him. I thought about what she said and I began talking to The Flame after school, later on, at the PAL. Then again I think I was just too distracted to stay mad at him because he had pizza. I mean come on, who can focus around pizza?

Anyway, that same night at the PAL, Amy and I met this kid named Dre. Dre was a friend of The Flame. He was very good looking, and he just so happened to be around our age. Dre was nice and really cool but he didn't go to our school so I had never seen him before. He however seemed to have quite the effect on a few of the girls in my school. He left quite a memorable first impression because that same day he and The Flame hopped over the Community Center gate to catch the bus and they almost took my phone with them...

Long story short I got my phone back from The Flame before he got the chance to leave and Dre became a friend to both Amy and I that night.

I know,...weird how these friendship things work right? Just take someone's phone and you guys are basically best friends.

Notes:

_____

_____

_____

_____

_____

_____

_____

_____

_____

_____

_____

Chapter 12: "I'm over him..."

Chapter 12:
"I'm over him..."

I guess you can say The Flame and I had patched things up, and I was unfortunately back to liking him...again. To be honest I never really stopped liking him though. I just hadn't liked what he'd done. I could never stay mad at the guy...

Anyway, I had begun talking to Jace a bit more since we hadn't spoken in a while and since I was over Jace I was very casual with our conversations. I treated him like a friend. However, just as I started talking to him as a friend, he had begun flirting with me. It was weird and typically something I should have expected him to do. Just as I'm over him completely, he starts flirting with me.

One time at lunch, when I was sitting with Zach and them again something I hadn't expected to happen happened. I was sitting on the opposite side of The Flame and Zach and Jack were teasing me like the annoying frycks they could occasionally be. They were repeatedly saying my name but the thing was they were adding The Flame's last name behind it. Now they knew The Flame had a girlfriend but sometimes they would act as if he didn't. While they consistently called me by The Flame's last name, The Flame pretended as if he didn't hear them, and he silently continued eating his lunch. That was until he decided to join in on the action and instead of calling me by his last name he called me by Jace's.

He watched my reaction to what he had just said and I immediately blushed and got quiet. I didn't even know that he knew about the whole Jace thing. I think Jace told a couple people though because some of the other 8th graders started asking me about it. Anyway I had made a mental note to ask The Flame how he knew about Jace later on, and I did after lunch.

As he was walking me to my language arts class, like he sometimes did after lunch, I asked him. I was kind of nervous though so I stuttered out a sentence along the lines of, "So who told you about Jace and me?"

His eyes that were once facing forward were now looking at me and his eyebrows furrowed, and he responded by asking me a question of his own, "So there's a thing between Jace and you?"

"No!" I quickly shouted. "What I meant to say is who told you about the Jace...and... me thing?" I didn't know how exactly to put what I was trying to say in words...now that I think about it I don't think I knew what I was trying to say at all. I was confused!

69

"I don't know," was his response, as he smirked mischievously.

So he wasn't going to tell me. Great.

Notes:

Essynce E. Moore

Chapter 13: "My first kiss"

Chapter 13:
"My first kiss"

For some reason I was always into the whole "first kiss" thing. To me, it was a part of growing up, a childhood memory that we could look back on years from now when we're flipping through an old yearbook or reuniting with old friends. I liked the idea of having a first kiss. Then again, I've only ever seen it happen on TV, and movies have an interesting way of making realistic events unrealistic.

I wanted my first kiss to be that year in 7th grade because that's when my cousin/sister had hers.

Anyway, I remember once when we were outside for recess, after lunch we were lined up against the school building, waiting to go back inside. There were a lot of us and we were all bunched up to the point where it didn't even look like a line. The Flame was standing in front of me and we were playfully teasing each other like we usually did and he began moving forward, pushing me back, as if to intimidate me.

74

However, my arms were crossed and I remained confident, with my head held high and a smirk on my face, just like there was on his. We were now really close, and my back was pressed up against the school building, with him in front of me. We kind of just looked at each other's eyes for a minute before he looked at my lips and then soon pulled away.

It was almost as if he snapped back into reality and remembered something...or someone. My guess is his girlfriend.

That same week, around 8:00 at night I received a phone call from an 8th grader who went by the name Danny. Danny and I were...I don't even know. I want to say we were friends but the guy flirted with me so much that in his eyes I think he saw us as something more than that. I found it kind of funny though. Earlier that day Danny had asked me if I liked him and I said yeah...as a friend, and he responded by saying okay. I got that question from Danny quite often though... It was almost as if he thought my answer would change within every hour.

I was used to his questions though. Everyday he'd either ask me if I liked him or if I wanted to kiss him. (Btw I always said no). Now, don't get me wrong: Danny wasn't annoying or anything he was really funny and kind of adorable actually but I just didn't like him in that way. To me he was kind of like a little brother who just happened to be older than me.

Anyway, as I was saying I had gotten a call from Danny one night and that call had me literally laughing so hard, to the point where I didn't even know why I was laughing. The conversation started off with the guy once again asking me if I liked him and I said once again that I only liked him as a friend. Then I decided to turn the tables and I asked Danny if he liked me and his response was "That depends on whether or not you change your answer." I laughed a little at his response and that's when the conversation got more...interesting.

Danny began not asking but telling me that the next day, at school he would kiss me. The guy had the whole thing planned out, where in the school he would kiss me, how he would kiss me, and even what he would do if I tried to fight back. All I did was laugh and tell him that that would only happen in his little 8th grade dreams. Honestly though, there was still a part of me that was a little worried that Danny would actually follow through with his little...plan. I did not want that guy to be my first kiss.

Anyway, I had to tell someone what had just happened between Danny and I so I texted Jacky after my conversation with him and told her everything that happened, and the next day at school, when everyone had a little time before homeroom I went to the hallway everyone would usually hang out in, in the morning. The Flame happened to be there and I went over and spoke to him for a little bit. That's when I saw Amy and I literally yanked her towards my direction and told her in her ear everything that happened the previous night, involving Danny. She yelled a very loud "WHAT?!" and I think her jaw had literally hit the floor. I told her that that happened to be the reason that I was trying to stay close to The Flame that morning. For some weird reason I kind of just knew he wouldn't let Danny...take action. Speaking of The Flame he heard Amy when she screamed that very loud "what" and he asked us what was going on. Amy ended up pulling him to the side and telling him. She also asked him if he had my back, and he said he did...and if I'm being honest here, the reassurance he had in his voice when he said that surprised me a little, he was just so...I don't even know. Let's just say I knew nothing was going to happen with Danny and that day nothing did.

Notes:

_____

_____

_____

_____

_____

_____

_____

_____

_____

_____

_____

_____

Chapter 14:

"I watched in horror as my fish were thrown..."

Chapter 14:
"I watched in horror as my fish were thrown..."

Now when you hear the words "goldfish" and "cupcakes" what do you think of? Now some may think of the actual fish with gills. Others may think of two snacks commonly eaten all over the globe. Here's what I think of...

- School

- Lunch

- Garbage Can

- Shocked Faces

- This is why I think of these things...

At the beginning of May, sometime near the 8th, it happened to be one of my friend's birthday. The friend's name was Bridget and I believe she was turning 13. Bridget and I had known each other since kindergarten and we had a pretty good relationship. We didn't have any classes together so we didn't get to talk so much but we did say hey to one-another and made small talk at lunch or in the halls. Anyway, Bridget had brought in cupcakes to celebrate her birthday and at lunch, she happened to be giving them out. I went over to the table she usually sat at during lunch and told her happy birthday. Now that may sound like a simple task, probably because the majority of the time it is, but in reality it was definitely one of those "easier said than done" moments. Multiple 7th graders crowded around Bridget and her vanilla and chocolate cupcakes, practically begging from the bottom of their hearts to get one. Some of them were people who barely knew Bridget and they began talking to her as if they were old friends. Typical, acting an entirely different way towards someone when a person has something they want. Anyway, that's not the point. That day at lunch I got a cupcake from Bridget and so did The Flame. I was sitting at the table with him and a couple other people, one of them being Jack. I had a pack of goldfish with me and I sat it next to my vanilla cupcake on the lunch table. Now if you went to school with me then you'd know that every day at lunch I would always get a pack of goldfish crackers from the vending machine. It had become like a routine for me, right when the lunch bell rang I'd rush to the machine before there was a line and I'd grab a pack of 60 cent goldfish.

The Flame, Zach, and Jack were used to me coming to our table everyday with goldfish and they had begun telling me that if I kept eating them I'd turn in to one. For some reason it seemed to really bug them. However, I'd just ignore them and eat my fish happily while they would occasionally try to take them away from me like the frycks they were.

That day when I had finished my cupcake I opened my pack of goldfish and out of the blue The Flame snatched them away from me with a devious smirk on his face. I watched in horror as my fish were thrown to Jack. The Flame had gestured towards the garbage can that happened to be only a few feet away and I witnessed my poor fish being tossed into the trash.

Thanks a lot Jack...please do note the sarcasm. Now everyone who knows me knows I take my food very seriously and The Flame would intentionally mess with me when I had food just to irritate me.

Zach sympathetically patted my shoulder and told me that they were doing me a favor and then he said all this other mumbo jumbo about him not wanting me to turn into a goldfish.

Some best friend I have...

A look of shock had crossed my face and it was in that moment I realized that was 60 cents I would never get back...however I did get back something. Something very well-known as revenge. Because it was The Flame who originally caused the trashing of my snack I decided to seek my vengeance on him. While, he peacefully ate his cupcake from Bridget I got up from the table and yanked the delicious treat away from him and headed towards the garbage can in which my snack was previously assassinated and thrown into. All eyes were on me and before anyone had the chance to stop me I threw The Flame's half-eaten cupcake into the can of junk and disgrace, also known as the garbage.

I then turned around with a satisfied grin on my face. Everyone at the table began laughing...everyone but The Flame whose mouth hung slightly open and looked to be in absolute shock.

What goes around comes around frycker. Let that be a lesson to us all.

Notes:

_____

_____

_____

_____

_____

_____

_____

_____

_____

_____

Chapter 15:
"A kiss, a Danny, and an innocent victim of a crush..."

Chapter 15:
"A kiss, a Danny, and an innocent victim of a crush..."

The end of the year was only a few blocks away and that's when some of the simple minded had begun to expect peace. However, my school knows of no peace.

Sometime in late May, for some random reason I hadn't sat at the table with the guys and Jacky like I usually did and that particular day there, at that table, there'd been a food fight. A harmless one, but still a food fight. One big enough that it caused everyone who was near the scene to vanish before accusation but small enough that one janitor at most was enough to clean it up. All I remember seeing was orange peels and fruit cups being thrown but honestly I don't know. Let's just say I made sure I kept my distance from the fruit salad at war.

By the time I'd gotten to class after lunch, all of my friends were talking about the mini food fight and the trouble the guys would get in if they got busted. The class erupted into a conversation on how The Flame, Jack, and the others were always up to something and that's when my friends had begun joking around and telling me to "keep your bae under control."

Later on that week something from the not-so-distant past had come right back to haunt me. Something involving a kiss, a Danny, and an innocent victim of a crush...

Notes:

_____

_____

_____

_____

_____

_____

_____

_____

_____

_____

_____

Chapter 16:
"Not.Gonna.Hap pen."

Chapter 16:
"Not.Gonna.Happen."

I believe it was a Thursday or Friday when I'd invited a couple friends over after school. I'd invited my close friend Mike, Jace, and Danny. For most of the time they were over everything went pretty smoothly I guess. We watched TV, had some snacks, and just chilled. Mike and Jace spent some of their time on their phones while Danny and I watched cartoons (told you I loved cartoons). Anyway, after about an hour and a half, the guys had to go and as they made their way out the door I hugged them all goodbye. Danny was the last one I'd hugged and right when the others were out the door he'd grabbed my face, closed his eyes, puckered his lips, and leaned in. For about 2.5 seconds I was in shock and that's when the heavens had decided to show me some mercy and give me my right to move back.

And with only a second to spare before Danny's lips were on mine I quickly covered his mouth and said these exact words:

"Not. Gonna. Happen."

I guess you could say I took my first kiss very seriously too. Seriously, enough to kindly kick Danny out right after. Don't worry though, till this day Danny and I are still just friends. Just how I like it.

Essynce E. Moore

Notes:

_____

_____

_____

_____

_____

_____

_____

_____

_____

_____

Chapter 17:

"I was a good girl gone bad..."

Chapter 17:
"I was a good girl gone bad..."

For a while everything seemed to be...normal. There was no drama, chaos, not even a fight, which for my school was a pretty big accomplishment. That "normal" lifestyle lasted up until...lunch. It was ruined when the principal called my mom to the school...

In school, I hung out with what people would commonly refer to as "the bad kids, the ones who always got in trouble." To me they were, really cool, fun, and different people. Where as to others they were "challenged." Anyway, because I hung out with these people who were my friends, we'd sit at lunch together and do what friends typically do; talk, laugh, and crack jokes. It was always the vice principal who was the chaperone for our grade during lunch but the day he was absent our principal, Mr. Parker, took his place.

Mr. Parker and I always had a good bond. He respected me and I respected him. He encouraged me as an entrepreneur and I encouraged him as our principal. But that day when he saw me sitting at the lunch table with my friends, something was...different. He gave me this weird look that read all kinds of emotions. His face read confusion, shock, and...disappointment. I was always a good kid but you'd think I was a good girl gone bad judging by the look on his face.

That same day, after lunch, as I was walking with The Flame to my language arts class I saw Mr. Parker again and that same look was on his face. Geez, I didn't seriously hurt anyone.

Anyway, The Flame and I went our separate ways and as I was about to walk into my class I saw the one person who's managed to scare me my entire life with just a look, the same person who makes me clean my room, and occasionally do the dishes. I saw my mom!

Notes:

_____

_____

_____

_____

_____

_____

_____

_____

_____

_____

Chapter 18:

"...someone I wasn't raised to be."

Chapter 18:
"...someone I wasn't raised to be."

Now when I saw my mom, don't get me wrong I was surprised but I wasn't as scared or terrified as you're probably thinking I was. I went over to my mom and she looked confused. Confused as to why the principal even called her to the school. Later on, I ended up finding out that my principal had emailed my mom, not even telling her why she really was contacted. He sent her an email stating that he was "concerned" about me and all this other mumbo jumbo. Honestly, though I was just mad that this big deal was seriously being made out of nothing. I had frycken lunch with my frycken friends! It was nothing to make a fuss about. Then again, even though I was mad I masked my anger and waited with my mom till Mr. Parker came around and took us to his office for a "meeting." In other words a test to see if I happened to be going down the wrong path.

During our little chat Mr. Parker explained to my mom what happened and in reality even my mom knew who I hung out with. She knew the people I hung out with personally. They'd been over my house countless times and they respected my mom just like they respected me. For the rest of the meeting Mr. Parker was reassured that I was staying focused and not getting off track, while I was forcing myself to not roll my eyes and be disrespectful. I mean the man had my mom worried for something that at the time I felt was stupid and immature. I had felt untrusted and was being treated like I was a bad kid, someone I wasn't raised to be. I was disappointed in my principal, like I had been disappointed in Amy for letting her boyfriend get to her and myself when I left Chris when he was upset.

Eventually I got over it though. Everyone I'd told the story, of what happened, told me that Mr. Parker really was just looking out for me and even though I didn't understand then, I understand now. He was only trying to help, just in a way I wasn't exactly accustomed to. It was really nothing to make such a big deal of. After all the end of the school year was only a short chapter away.

Notes:

_____

_____

_____

_____

_____

_____

_____

_____

_____

_____

_____

_____

—————————————

Chapter 19:

"A day I didn't want to forget."

—————————————

Chapter 19:
"A day I didn't want to forget."

There was about a month of school left and one day when the end of the day bell rang I went over to the store by my school, like everyone else did every day. There we would either go to the store, meet up with friends to walk with, or get picked up. Earlier that Friday afternoon my friend Mike and I had planned to hangout after school, he'd be inviting The Flame and I had my close friend Faith who'd be joining us. Faith didn't go to our school but everyone at our school knew her and she knew them because she had been in our school district up until 7th grade. However, she still lived in town and she sometimes would come by our school afterwards.

Anyway, this particular day Faith, The Flame, Mike, and I would go to my house to simply hangout. I knew my mom would be cool with it because she knew all of them and they all loved her. All of my friends loved her as if she were their mom. So by the time we had walked to my house we started watching TV, talking, and just chilling. That's when my mom rushed down the stairs that lead to where we were, in the living room, and told me that I had an event that day that she had forgotten about. She rushed me to my room to get ready and after I was dressed I finally managed to ask her where my friends would go and she said they would just have to come with us.

We all rushed to the car and that's when my friends and I remembered that we had ordered Chinese so my mom hesitantly rushed us to our local Chinese spot and I quickly got out, grabbed our food, and we were off. My mom explained to me that I'd be speaking to some girls and answering their questions about my first book, 6th Grade Middle School Chronicles and I was pretty much ready to go. I was used to this kind of thing, events had become second nature to me. Even ones that were last minute or in this case, unintentionally forgotten about.

When we got to the event, my friends took a seat, my mom stood by them, and I did my thing as they all watched. Now this may seem "boring" or "uninteresting" but this day meant a lot to me. It was one of the first real times my friends had seen me do my thing. They got to see what I did in my daily life outside of school, and that meant a lot to me. My friends were important to me and I always wanted them to be involved in what I did. So that day I marked as a memory, in this book, as a day I didn't want to forget.

After the event, we ate the Chinese food I had paid for in the car, and my mom dropped The Flame, Faith, and I off to the pal like we'd asked. Mike had basketball practice and my mom took him to wherever that was and later on I ended up finding out that Mike had gotten them lost on the way. My mom and I ended up laughing about it.

While Faith, The Flame, and I were at the pal we had a conversation that felt like it would last forever. A good kind of forever. Faith and I ended up talking about this guy she used to like and at the time I was convinced she still liked him.

"I can see it...it's like an invisible spark between you too," I said. "That's what I see between you and The Flame."

The Flame and I looked at each other for a moment...neither of us saying anything. But then I looked away because I couldn't look anymore. I guess I was confused and curious as to how others could see that "invisible spark" and we couldn't. I used to be able to see it but after he started dating girlfriend number two I had begun to think that he didn't see it anymore so I thought why should I. I told Faith that he had a girlfriend as a way of saying there was no point in believing there was some spark between us and that's when he interrupted and said he no longer was taken.

Later on, when Faith had begun having a conversation with the guy I thought she still liked, who had recently arrived I went over by the swings. I just sat there swinging and thinking about everything and that's when something happened. I always thought that when you were sitting alone, it would always be important to remember the person who came and sat next to you. I believed that the individual who reaches out to you says a lot about that person. It shows that they care about you, because when you're alone and they decide to change that, in my opinion, it's their way of saying "I care about you too much to let you sit alone."

So when I was alone on the swings, watching everyone do their own thing, I remembered when out of all people it was The Flame who came and stood next to me. We talked and teased each other while he pushed me lightly on the swing and that right there was a moment I would never forget.

The day ended with Faith going home, and The Flame and another one of my friends all joining me at my house around 8:00 pm, which was my curfew, to hangout more. There we watched movies and play fought with my boxing gloves. It was really fun and eventually around 10:00 pm the two were picked up. That simple day was definitely one I didn't want to forget.

Notes:

_____

_____

_____

_____

_____

_____

_____

_____

_____

_____

_____

Chapter 20: "An End."

Chapter 20:
"An End."

The long school year had finally come to an end. Our last day of 7th grade ended with nothing but fun in every class. No work was given, thank goodness, and no drama was displayed. Everyone was in the best mood they had been in all year. Could you blame them?

We'd soon be having a two-month break from all the drama and dating. Soon we wouldn't have homework or quizzes due. For two months we'd get to be kids. Kids with freedom. For two months it would be summer, full of games and toys and laughs and fun. Just like in that movie Sharkboy and Lavagirl!

However, I'm getting a little ahead of myself because right after those two incredible months I'd be brought right back to my friends, my school, and The Flame. And if there's one thing I learned this year is that I cannot see the future and I never know what chronicles it has in store for me. Then again, 8th grade couldn't possibly be as dramatic and unpredictable as this year, right?

Oh Essynce, if only you could see the future...

The End

Notes:

_____

_____

_____

_____

_____

_____

_____

_____

_____

_____

7th Grade

Middle School Chronicles

"Oh Essynce, if only you could see the future...."

Written by

Essynce E. Moore

The Fashionista

Essynce Moore started designing clothes at the tender age of 6 with just for fun doodles in her school binder and notepads. Her passion was and still is, to find her own style and to share her creative UPSCALE clothing ideas and styles with youth around the world. Essynce is now a "TEEN" that had turned her passion into a business at the age of 10 in 2013, with the launch of her official clothing line branded Essynce Couture, LLC with the motto "*a child's passion for fashion.*" Essynce Couture also has a natural body product line for children, tweens, and teens labeled "Wynk" by Essynce Couture. In 2015 Essynce launched Essynce Couture Spa and Boutique EXCLUSIVELY for Children, Tweens, and Teens to give the youth a place of their own to visit and be pampered, inspired, and educated.

Essynce is an entrepreneur, child's fashion designer/stylist, author, actress, celebrity, motivational speaker, and fashionista that brings a positive vibe to her peers and others. She's been in numerous fashion shows, pageants, karate tournaments and has spoken at numerous conferences and/or workshops. In 2016-17 Essynce is in the following movies: King of Newark, Custody, and Darker than Blue, and Maggie's Plan. She has SHOWCASED at both NY Fashion Weeks and Atlanta Kids Fashion Week while also ripping the runway. She's released her first book 6th Grade Middle School Chronicles in 2015 and has been featured on BET, Verizon Fios News, BlackNews.com, MadameNoire, The Record newspaper and a host of other news and media outlets 2015-2016. Essynce has also been awarded and received proclamations by The City of Passaic and the State of New Jersey – Senate and General Assembly upon the auspicious occasion of the Grand Opening of her business Essynce Couture Spa and Boutique, LLC in 2015 in the City of Passaic. In 2014 she was interviewed and featured on NBC (Channel 4 News), Jeff Foxx of WBLS FM, BuzzFeed, Yahoo, Verizon Fios Channel 1 News, NBC Channel 4 News, she was awarded "2014 Young Emerging Leader" by Alpha Kappa Alpha, she's been featured in the 2013 TIME for Kids Magazine, Honored 2013 Entrepreneur of the Year by the Vashti School for Future Leaders, she's been seen on the Uncle Majic Commercial (BET, VH1, Channel 11, etc), HBO (Bored to Death), and has involved herself with a host of other events and projects.

Essynce is also a member of the New York Youth Chamber of Commerce (NYYCC).

This young "phenomenon" is *BUZZING* and she can't wait to see children being pampered, as well as, wearing her Essynce Couture brand all around the world.

The Essynce Couture Brand

What makes us unique?!? Essynce Couture, LLC is one of the 1st children's clothing lines designed by a child with "education" in mind. We focus on styling our clothes to compliment all sizes, races, and colors of all children around the world. In addition, we offer great incentives through our Essynce Couture membership program to the children who support Essynce Couture, LLC by allowing them the opportunity to show and prove. They can upload either their report cards, certificates, awards or any other form of achievement(s) to one of the Essynce Couture social networks (instagram, twitter, or facebook) and may be selected to be rewarded by Essynce Couture, LLC incentives. This will encourage children to continue to do well in school and remind them that education is very important, rewarding, stylish, and can be fun!

www.essyncecouture.com

Anonymous Unexpected Moments

During my 7th grade chronicle I experienced the unexpected. No person or thing failed to surprise me. However, I was not the only one who was hit by the unfathomable circumstance of reality. I went around and asked some of my friends what happened to them in 7th grade that wasn't predicted. I got some interesting responses and well...here they are!

I didn't expect...

1. When I made the basketball team
2. The time I almost got jumped
3. I went camping and almost died
4. The best friendship I've had in my whole life
5. My behavior to change
6. Having a good relationship with my teachers
7. I didn't think I would have such a good bond with one of my friends from last year
8. I would lose so many friends over 1 boy
9. I didn't expect to get in a fight with

someone I barely knew and then later on become friends with them

10. I didn't expect for me to fall in love (I did expect my glo up though lol)

11. I didn't expect there to be a fight almost everyday

12. I didn't expect to like this guy

13. I didn't expect to not make honor roll

My personal unexpected moment:

14. I didn't expect to learn so much about the world, my friends, and myself. I learned that when it comes to the world what we can see is less than half of what there is out there. I learned that all my friends have problems whether it has to do with their grades, personal lives, or heartbreak. Finally, I learned that 7th grade was the most dramatic, overrated, heartbreaking school year of my life...for now.

Notes:

_____

_____

_____

_____

_____

_____

_____

_____

_____

_____

_____

_____

CPSIA information can be obtained
at www.ICGtesting.com
Printed in the USA
LVOW10s1541281117
557886LV00012B/1016/P